W9-CNA-981

1100   1200   1300   1400   1500   1600   1700   1800   1900   2000

CANADA THROUGH TIME
Canada Today

Kathleen Corrigan

capstone

Read Me is published by Heinemann Raintree,
an imprint of Capstone Press,
1710 Roe Crest Drive, North Mankato, Minnesota 56003

© 2016 Heinemann-Raintree
an imprint of Capstone Global Library, LLC
Chicago, Illinois

To contact Capstone please visit www.mycapstone.com

All rights reserved. No part of this publication may be reproduced or transmitted in any form or by any means, electronic or mechanical, including photocopying, recording, taping, or any information storage and retrieval system, without permission in writing from the publisher.

Edited by James Benefield
Designed by Philippa Jenkins
Original illustrations © Capstone Global Library Ltd 2016
Picture research by Kelly Garvin
Production by Victoria Fitzgerald
Originated by Capstone Global Library Limited
Printed and bound in China

ISBN 978 1 410 98122 6 (hardback)
19 18 17 16 15
10 9 8 7 6 5 4 3 2 1

ISBN 978 1 410 98127 1 (paperback)
19 18 17 16 15
10 9 8 7 6 5 4 3 2 1

ISBN 978 1 410 98132 5 (ebook)

Acknowledgments
Photo credits: Capstone Press/Karon Dubke, 28, 29; Getty Images: ANDRE FORGET/AFP, 15, Colin McConnell/Toronto Star, 17, Education Images/UIG, 19, Jerry Kobalenko, 5, Universal History Archive/UIG, 12, Steve Russell/Toronto Star, 13, Tom Szczerbowski, 23; Newscom/W8 Media/Splash News, 21; Science Source/Planet Observer, 10; Shutterstock: 2009fotofriends, cover (top), 9 (top left), BGSmith, 9 (bottom right), Chad Zuber, 9 (top right), erandamx, 7, FER737NG 14, gary yim, cover (bottom), James Wheeler, 9 (bottom left), Jason Cheever, 11, Jeff Whyte, 16, Jiri Flogel, 27, Matthew Jacques, 8, meunierd, 25, Norman Pogson, 6, Sergei Bachlakov, 20, Sven Hoppe, 22, Thomas Barrat, 24, V.J. Matthew, 18, Vladimer Sazonov, 26

Every effort has been made to contact copyright holders of any material reproduced in this book. Any omissions will be rectified in subsequent printings if notice is given to the publisher.

All the Internet addresses (URLs) given in this book were valid at the time of going to press. However, due to the dynamic nature of the Internet, some addresses may have changed, or sites may have changed or ceased to exist since publication. While the author and publisher regret any inconvenience this may cause readers, no responsibility for any such changes can be accepted by either the author or the publisher.

Some words are shown in bold, **like this**. You can find out what they mean by looking in the glossary.

Contents

Canada today

Canada crosses the **continent** of North America. It has more land than any country in the world except for Russia. About 35 million people live in Canada. Most people live in cities and towns. Some Canadians live in **rural** communities or in small **settlements** in the far north.

Canada has ten **provinces** and three **territories.**

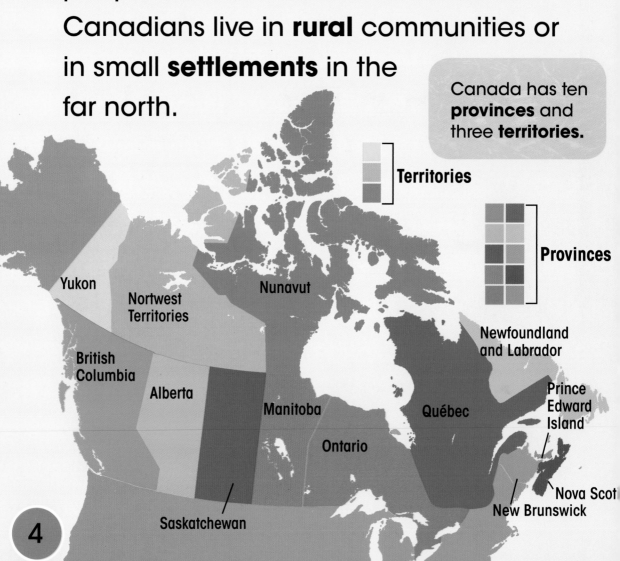

Territories

Provinces

Yukon

Nortwest Territories

Nunavut

British Columbia

Alberta

Manitoba

Québec

Ontario

Newfoundland and Labrador

Prince Edward Island

Nova Scot

New Brunswick

Saskatchewan

DID YOU KNOW?

The military base Canadian Forces Station Alert is farther north than any other settlement in the world. It is 817 km (508 miles) from the geographic North Pole.

Cities

The **capital city** of Canada is Ottawa. Each **province** and **territory** has its own capital city too. The five biggest cities in Canada are Toronto, Montréal, Vancouver, Ottawa, and Calgary. Nearly 15 million people live in these areas. That is more than one third of the people living in Canada. Around 2.8 million people live in the biggest city, Toronto.

Most of the Canadian government is in Ottawa.

One of the most famous buildings in Toronto is the CN Tower.

Land and climate

Canada has many types of land. There are high mountains in the west and lower mountains in the east. There are prairie grasslands, forests, and arctic **tundra**. Canada also has different **climates**. Some places, like Victoria, B.C., get very little snow in the winter. Some places in the Arctic are always frozen.

Only low plants with short roots can survive in the tundra.

DID YOU KNOW?

Most people in Canada live in the south, where it is warmer.

Water

Canada has about 2 million lakes. It has more lakes than any other country in the world. The biggest lakes are the Great Lakes, between Canada and the United States. There are also oceans on three sides of Canada: the Atlantic, the Pacific, and the Arctic oceans.

The Great Lakes have 18 percent of the world's fresh water in them.

Canada has fresh water **glaciers** in the mountains and on many islands in the Arctic.

Many people

The first people in Canada were the **Aboriginal** people. European people arrived in Canada from the 1500s. Today, most people living in Canada were born there. About 20 percent were born in other countries. **Immigrants** come from every part of the world to live in Canada safely and happily.

Aboriginal people settled in Canada over 10,000 years ago.

DID YOU KNOW?

Before 1970, most immigrants
to Canada came from Europe.
Since then, most immigrants
have come from Asia.

Languages

The two **official languages** in Canada are English and French. Most people in Canada speak one official language. Some people speak both. Many other languages are spoken in Canada. Some people speak an **Aboriginal** language. Many **immigrants** still speak the language they spoke before arriving.

In some parts of Canada, street signs use both official languages.

DID YOU KNOW?

The **territory** of Nunavut has four official languages – English, French, Inuktitut, and Inuinnaqtun. Inuktitut and Inuinnaqtun are **Inuit** languages. The sign in the picture above is in English and Inuktitut.

Off to school

Most children go to school for about ten months each year. They have a long summer holiday. Many people go to college or university after they finish high school. Some people become **apprentices** and learn while they work.

Some students go to very big schools. Others go to tiny schools.

Canadian children usually start school when they are between four and five years old.

Canadian workers

There are many different jobs in Canada. Many people work outside. For example, some people are loggers or miners, or they catch fish or farm. There are many jobs inside, too. Some are health care workers or have jobs in factories, stores, and restaurants. Other Canadians are scientists or school teachers.

Some Canadians work on oil rigs, such as this one.

DID YOU KNOW?

Fishing is a major industry in Canada. Thousands of Canadians have fishing industry jobs.

Entertainment

Canadians do many things for fun. Many people enjoy music, films, and TV. Some people like to garden or fix cars. Many Canadians like to play board games, card games, video games, and sports. They also love to watch movies and TV shows, and go on nature walks.

Canadians often get together for special events like a Pow Wow or a Chinese New Year parade.

DID YOU KNOW?

Many Canadians are successful authors, musicians, actors, and artists. For example, Shania Twain is famous outside Canada.

The Cirque du Soleil began in Québec in 1984.

21

Sports

Canadians love sports. In the summer people play soccer, baseball, tennis, golf, and other games. In the winter, Canadians ski, snowboard, curl, and play ice hockey. There are many wonderful places for people to swim, canoe, or hike in Canada. Canadians also play many indoor sports, such as basketball and volleyball.

Many Canadians enjoy watching hockey games, which are exciting.

DID YOU KNOW?

Canada has two national sports: lacrosse in the summer and ice hockey in the winter. Lacrosse began as an **Aboriginal** game.

Landmarks

Canada has many special or beautiful **landmarks**. Some of the most famous are:

- Niagara Falls and the CN Tower in Ontario
- The Rocky Mountains in Alberta and British Columbia
- Old Québec City (Vieux- Québec)
- The Bay of Fundy between New Brunswick and Nova Scotia
- The Confederation Bridge

Tourists go to see the polar bears near Churchill, Manitoba, in October and November.

The old city of Québec
(Vieux-Québec) has
many beautiful buildings.

Canadian symbols

Maple trees and their leaves are symbols of Canada. A red maple leaf is on the Canadian flag. Maple syrup, a Canadian treat, comes from maple trees. Canadian coins show many symbols of Canada. Most coins have animal symbols such as the loon, polar bear, caribou, or beaver.

Many Canadian children learn about Canadian money by talking about the pictures on the coins.

DID YOU KNOW?

Canada's national anthem "O Canada" became the official anthem in 1980. That was 100 years after it was first sung.

A symbols collage

Canada, its **provinces**, and **territories** all have many symbols. Why not make a collage of some of them?

What you need:

- a list of symbols for your province or territory and the symbols of Canada
- paper
- scissors
- a piece of cardboard
- real things such as coins or a maple leaf
- glue

What to do:

1. Draw the symbols on some paper or print pictures of them from the Internet. You might have some pictures you draw and some printed pictures.

2. Cut out the pictures.

3. Cover the piece of cardboard with your pictures. You could overlap some pictures or put some on sideways or upside down. You can add some real objects too. Make it interesting to look at.

4. When you are happy with your collage, glue each piece on carefully. Be sure to use enough glue to make everything lie flat.

5. Display your collage.

Glossary

Aboriginal original and ancestors of the people who live in a land; in Canada, this includes the Inuit and the Métis people

apprenticeship special training period

capital city place where the government meets

climate weather in a place over many years

continent vast land area containing different countries and nationalities

glacier big layer of ice slowly moving over land

immigrant person who moves to a new country

Inuit Aboriginal people who live in northern Canada

landmark special building, place, or monument

official language main language used by the government and people

province section of the country with its own government, whose power is granted by the Constitution Act

rural countryside; outside cities and towns

settlement place where different people live

territory section of the country with its own local government that is given power by the federal government

tundra vast, treeless plain in the Arctic where there is always a frozen layer below the soil

Find out more

Books

The Kids Book of Canada, Barbara Greenwood (Kids Can Press, 2007)

Wow Canada!: Exploring this Land from Coast to Coast to Coast, Vivien Bowers (Maple Tree, 2010)

Websites

FactHound offers a safe, fun way to find Internet sites related to this book. All of the sites on FactHound have been researched by our staff.

Here's all you do:

Visit www.facthound.com
Type in this code: 9781410981226

Index